Title Of Book
TOUGH CONVERSATIONS AT WORK

Book Subtitle
7 MAGIC TIPS AND TRICKS OF
DEALING WITH DIFFICULT
CONVERSATIONS AT WORK

Table of Contents

Introduction

This book contains proven steps and strategies on how to have tough workplace conversations. Difficult conversations within any setting are a challenge for everyone, and some people make every effort to avoid them altogether. Tough conversations can have a profound impact on your career, happiness, and future. With the right skills and tools, anyone can feel confident handling tough conversations. You can master the art of tough conversations, and this guide will show you an efficient way to. This book provides you necessary tools and skills needed to handle tough conversations confidently and escape every conversational quicksand that may attempt to drown your confidence.

Tough conversations are part of every professional's life, irrespective of his/her desire. This manuscript will gift you the wisdom and confidence to deal with every tough conversation with ease. With the skills you learn in this guide, you will never have to worry about the outcome of an important conversation again. This tough conversation guide also gives you the tools you need to step up to life's most difficult and important conversations Say what is on your mind and achieve your desired result. This motivational, inspirational, and practical handbook describes a surefire way to increase the confidence and competence of professionals who need it.

Chapter 1 The Elements of Conversation

A conversation is an exchange by people with an interest in pleasant discourse. A conversation involves exchanging of words and ideas. If one person directs the arena, the conversation becomes a presentation, an oration, or a lecture. Besides the words, a conversation comprises facial expressions, gestures, the tone of voice, body language and volume. This is why emails are not conversation. Conversation results in a new relationship, a new idea, a new understanding of people or concepts, or a new product or service.

The "something new" requirement removes many types of communication from the realm of conversation. Good conversation requires authenticity; you can't fake respect for very long. If you don't like people or really don't care much about what they think and believe, you won't be much of a conversationalist. Trust is the most important conversational element. The conversation won't happen unless people feel comfortable sharing their thoughts and speaking their minds.

Here are some tips for fostering trust:

- o Don't rush. Delay if you must, but don't rush. If you are rushed, worried or angry, then you can't give full attention to your conversational partner.

- o Focus on the other person. You may be good at multitasking, but don't do it while you are having a conversation. Don't check your messages, answer your cell phone or answer questions when talking with another person.

- o Listen with intention: Not listening carefully to your conversation partner is plain rude.

Chapter 2 What it Means to Have a Tough Conversation

Fear can make your conversation difficult

No one escapes difficult conversations. Different people find different types of conversations trying. Different types of fear affect different people.

- o Fear of hurting someone's feelings or being hurt ourselves.

- o Fear of not being liked.

- o Fear of losing an important relationship.

- o Fear of being wrong.

- o Fear of looking stupid.

Fear, fight and flight

Fear has a profound effect on conversation. When we have to talk to a friend or co-worker about an unpleasant subject, the body responds as if we are in danger (such as we are about to get hit by a car). Our body prepares us to fight or to flee.

The fight or flight response is a life-saving mechanism that has come down to us from prehistory. Our ancestors faced physical danger, but today we mostly face mental assault. However, the fight or flee symptoms get us ready to defend ourselves from any type of assault.

Fight conversation reactions

The "fight" end of the spectrum includes several possible responses to the danger of an unpleasant conversation.

Aggression

Often when we get threatened, one of the most common fight reactions is to meet fire with fire – becoming aggressive. Such as:

"I would like to speak with you about several mistakes you made in the sales report."

"Why? I didn't make any mistakes! Ask others, they will testify to that."

Aggression is often accompanied by an increase in volume, inappropriate language, and belittling of others. Becoming aggrieve can be a good offense, but there is not much hope for the rest of this conversation.

Sarcasm

Sarcasm is a very common fight response. A sarcastic exchange might consist of words like this:

"What you think of this year's annual report?" "I wrote the whole thing."

Yes! "You showed improvement!" "I noticed only four typos in the whole report!"

Passive Aggression

Passive aggression is also a fight response.

"Well! Where is your report?" "You should have submitted yesterday?"

"I had to attend the office meeting yesterday, so I was unable to focus on the report. I will submit tomorrow."

"That won't be enough. The Chairman wants to do a complete assessment, and that report is needed today."

"Well, you should have reminded me."

Chapter 3 Asking for a Pay Raise

Whether you want a pay raise or want other benefits, asking for money or equivalent of money can be difficult. Knowing more about your situation and your job can make your request less stressful and increase your chances of getting a pay raise. Before you ask for a pay raise, you need to know what you want, your value in the market; whether your company can meet your demands and how your work has affected the company's business position.

What you want

If it is cash, have a figure or a percentage of the increase in mind. If it is not money related, then you can ask for more vacation time, a more distinguish job title or other things that are an appropriate reward for your contributions. You weaken your position if you waffle, and look confused and show a lack of confidence. Know exactly what you are going to ask for before you open your mouth.

The company's financial condition

When the company is profiting, you are in a better position to ask for more money. Remember, even if the market is up and economic indicators favorable, your company may be going through hard times.

Your market value

Your hiring process is the best time to address your salary concerns. Also, if you find out that you have undersold yourself at the beginning, then you can negotiate again. On the other hand, not asking for a just salary at the beginning can hurt you, and you may have to live with it for a while.

Your contributions to the successf

If you are only doing your job, then it is not enough. You need to outperform your expectations or create a successful extension of your company's business. Those are all the things you can cite as you make your case. Spend some time compiling your list of accomplishments and quantifying your contributions; numbers matter. For example:

- o "It was my idea to install the new automated barcode scanner system in the warehouse. It will reduce the time and save us money by lowering staff we need. It is estimated that the company will save around $20,000 because of this newly installed scanner."

- o "I changed the furniture coating and introduced a newer, model of coating, which will help the furniture last longer. Sales are increasing because of this improvement."

- o "I recommended that we replace the advertising campaign. The agency wanted the much cheaper public relations program. We received 19 mentions from the local media and 4 articles in national trade magazines. Furthermore, it cost $20,000 less than the advertising."

Non-quantifiable but valuable contributions might include:

- o "Several employees complained about headaches and mild flu symptoms. It was I who suggested them to take sick days instead of working and make it a serious health problem."

- o "Indoor planting and introduction of green images inside the office were my ideas. Several employees have told me, their productivity increased because of a more natural work environment."

Pay raise conversation example

Start by setting the tone of the conversation. Use appreciative, collegial, and warm tone, but avoid extra fluff. Instead of beating around the bush, go directly to the issue.

- o You: Hi David (Boss), thanks for meeting me today. I know you are really busy so I will go straight to the point. (You know how valuable your boss's time is and don't want to waste time.)

- o Boss: No problem. Please have a seat.

- o You: Thank you. So, I would like to first mention the variety of things I did for this company over the past 2 years.

- o (Before you ask for a raise, you bring up your contribution to the company to show your value to the company.) Your bosses are busy people, so they may not know your every contribution. Gently remind them, but don't brag.)

- o You: (with a smile and gentle voice) I like to discuss a pay raise/other benefit/ a promotion, etc.

- o Boss: OK, go ahead, but know that the final decision about the promotion/ pay raise not totally up to me. (You are familiar with this type of bureaucracy if you worked for a big company, so you are used to it. Don't get discouraged, mention your contribution to the company and ask for a pay raise.)

- o You: Here are the files showing I bought 8 new clients to the company, and 3 of them made multiple purchases. I exceed the target that was set and currently works on bringing bigger clients to the company.

- o Boss: Fantastic! You are doing great! Keep it up!

- o You: Thank you. My plan is to continue to bring new clients to the company who are likely to make big purchases. So I am thinking, a pay raise will boost my morale and motivate me to work harder.

- o Boss: Could you be more specific?

- o You: Sure, I think a 10% pay raise is just.

- o Boss: OK. I heard you; I will discuss this issue in the next HR meeting and let you know the results.

- o You: Great! I appreciate that.

Chapter 4 Conveying Bad News at Work

Delivering bad news

Life's only constant changes. People are receiving bad news every day. Companies close, benefits are slashed; pensions are abandoned. A beloved boss resigns; operations are altered; entire divisions are moving overseas, costing thousands of jobs and so on. If you are the person who has to deliver this life-changing news, then you should say it in a clear voice with compassion.

Rehearse

Bad news can be life-changing for the person who is getting it. So you can't be cavalier and offhand. Note the main points and rehearse what you have to say a couple of times. You don't want to sound rehearsed, but you want to make sure you are candid, accurate and compassionate.

Do it quickly

Once a bad story is released to the people, it is often distorted, embellished or transformed into something that is very dissimilar to the actual facts. To prevent it, you need to spread the facts as soon as possible. If you have to fire someone, say, "Bad news. We have to let you go," is enough. If you yammer on about deselection, involuntary attrition, growing down the workforce surplus or negative retention, then the worker may be very confused. It is cruel to keep them guessing, so go straight to the point. Not delivering the news, and dancing around the issue will only prolong the agony and can trigger more negative reaction than getting fired.

Get to the point

Much of the bad news that rain on downfalls on individual people. The managers and supervisors are required to deal with the situations one by one. If you have unpleasant facts to deliver, then go to the bad news right away with words such as:

o "Amanda, I am sorry, but the report you submitted is unsatisfactory, and you need to redo it by Monday."

o "John, your behavior towards the junior staff is not acceptable. Furthermore, this is not your first offense, so I am suspending you for one week."

o "Whitney, Your request for the additional day-time shift has been denied."

Stick to the facts

Organize your speech and enrich it with facts before you speak with your coworkers and employees. What were the reasons for denying Amanda's report? Point them out very specifically. If you can't mention the mistakes, Amanda can't improve. Make it clear why Whitney's request for the additional day-time shift has been rejected. Be honest. If the decision is final, then don't hint that there is hope, if they request again. Be firm and get the person ready to face reality.

Coping with strong reactions

No one wants to hear that they have to relocate to another state or get fired or they are not getting the promotion this year. Usually, reactions include denial, anger, and frustration:

- o "I have been a loyal employee for this company for the past three years, and you pull the rug out from under me like this?"

- o "I haven't got a promotion for the past three years. If I don't get promoted this year, then it will be too long."

- o "You have a responsibility to the company, but what about your responsibility to your hardworking employees?"

- o "I can't believe this is happening to me!"

They may yell, weep, swear at you or threaten suit. Don't mirror the other's emotions. Sit quietly and remain calm. Allow the person to vent. If the person appears to be confused or shocked, then ask a few questions to assure yourself that the message has gotten through:

- o "Have I been clear in what I have said?"

- o "You look confused. Is there anything you need me to say and clarify things?"

- o "Do you have more questions?"

Be empathetic

When delivering bad news, you are the only other person in the room, so you should expect some pushback. Do your best to show empathy and compassion even though you are the one who is announcing the tough decision. Say things to soften the blow, such as:

- o "I wish it weren't true, too."

o "It's a sad time."

o "I feel so bad about having to share this news."

o "I know this is hard to hear."

When and if it's appropriate, point the employee to sources to help: outplacement assistance, unemployment compensation or other resources.

End on an upbeat note

There are times when you can't put a good face on the news. If it is possible, ending your speech with an upbeat note can change the atmosphere of gloom and doom to hope and possibility. You can say:

o "I know it is a blow to you that your plan was rejected. But the chairman took the time to write you a letter to compliment you. He wouldn't have done it if he didn't think you have potential."

o "I know you were expecting a promotion after this merger. I am sure once we settle everything; you will get your promotion."

Telling the boss bad news

You have to tell the boss the bad news, but it also means it might get you fired. Now you have a dilemma.

Qualify the news

Does the news urgent? Does your boss need to know the news? The boss's responsibilities are to the entire company or department, so don't bring a minor problem to them. Try to solve minor problems at a lower level and only bring your boss the urgent news that needs their attention.

Get there first

When you made a blunder, it should be you who tell them about it. Don't wait for one of your coworkers to deliver the news (who's only intention is to get your job). Moreover, don't try to pass the news via e-mail because important news needs face-to-face discussion.

Discuss the details

Get your facts, figures and reasons prepared. "How you do not see this coming." Or "What are your reasons for failing" are types of questions you need to answer. Be ready to explain fully. Give your boss the complete picture and present data that supports your claim. Don't leave room for your boss to guess. Present facts so there is no room for speculation.

Take responsibility

Making a mistake doesn't make you a bad person, it shows that you are human. There are options open to you, such as you can say, "I am truly sorry for this error. I like to remedy it and I know how. Perhaps I can present you the solution later."

Have a plan

You made a mistake, but it doesn't mean you have to rush and deliver the news instantly. Sit and think about how you can improve the situation. Is any of the work is recoverable? Is there any way you can save the company some cost? Or do you have an idea on how to do it cost effectively the next time around?

Giving bad news to your team

Usually, you need to inform bad news to a single person. However, there are occasions where you need to inform your team bad news, such as the marketing plan they designed didn't deliver the expected results, or they missed their sales targets by a mile or the budget for their project has been cut 30%.

Keep it within the team

When the team made a mistake, only share the news who was involved in making it. Don't disclose the issue to those who were affected by it.

Keep it factual

Discuss all the facts surrounding the event. If necessary, arrange a slide show, but don't forget the actual message.

Keep it impersonal

Separate what was done from who did it. When having a team meeting, don't point fingers to an individual. If necessary, talk to that person later, separately.

If possible, keep it positive

Maybe the previous marketing plan didn't deliver. So is there some other plan that can work better? How about other group's success? Is there anything you and your group can learn from them?

Chapter 5 Dealing with Workplace Impoliteness

A vast majority of office workers believe that they have been subjected to impoliteness or outright bullying in the workplace. Most office workers say they have been:

o Gossiped about

o Given dirty looks

o Interrupted and/or disregarded when trying to make a valid point.

o Insulted

o Yelled at by co-workers or supervisors.

o Reprimanded in front of workmates

Impoliteness and rude behavior affect everyone, from manager to employee.

The cost of impoliteness

Employees getting harassed by a manager or other coworker suffer mental trauma. Data shows that harassed employees:

o Focus on how they are treated instead of working during the office hours.

o Waste time by plotting how to get back at the rude person.

o Take more sick days.

o Arrive late and leave early.

o Work slowly to take revenge.

o Resign.

o Inadvertent impoliteness

o Often rude behavior becomes so normal that those who indulge in them might not even consider them rude, but they are. For example, do you do any of the following?

o Continue to work when someone is speaking to you

o Forget to use "please" and "thank you"

o Neglect to identify yourself when calling others

o Introduce people only by the first name

o Call others by their first names while retaining your own title.

o Use a caller's or client's first name without getting permission.

o Swear in the office?

o Keep people on hold without reason

o Notify only the successful candidate for the job and forgot the rest.

o Neglect to return phone calls

Let's start with the last point

o Neglecting to return phone calls: You don't have to return sales calls, but you must call back to a business-related phone call. Don't tell people that you will call and then not make the call. Remember, even if you consider it a low priority, others may not. Same goes for e-mail.

o Neglecting to notify all job candidates: If you can't phone every candidate, then e-mail everyone to inform the results.

o Keeping people on hold: This is very rude. It can be seen a crude and boorish way to establishing a superior position. Plan your calls.

o Swearing: Impolite language is offensive to many people, and some consider it as a negative workplace behavior.

o Addressing others improperly: You can't mention your clients by their first name without permission. Ask for permission first and then mention them by their first name.

o Introducing others improperly: When introducing others mention both first and last names and some identifying information.

o Neglecting to identify yourself on the phone: For example,

   - "Good morning. Quality Communications; this is Frank Stein."

   - "Is Lex there?"

   - "May I ask who's calling?"

   - "Frank."

   - "Frank who?"

- "Frank N. Stein."

- "From?"

- "Cleveland."

- "Sir, may I have the name of the company?"

- "......."

o Forgetting to use your manners: Always use "Please" and "Thank you" when communicating with others. Remember, courtesy is never wrong and employees appreciate most.

o Working while others are speaking to you: Don't keep on working if someone is standing in front of your desk.

Confronting rudeness

Cool off first

When you have been provoked or brushed off, you may be tempted to be equally provocative to use bitterness and sarcasm to make your point. It will only make things worse. The idea is to stop the impoliteness. To remove yourself from the situation, walk away with dignity; go to a place where you will be alone. Take a breather and prepare your approach.

Speak directly

Don't rely on third-party or send hints. Speak directly to the person who was impolite to you and doesn't water down what you want to say. Express in firm tone such as "I need to clear the air on an important issue." Or "I have something I need to discuss with you." Avoid opening with "What do you have against me?" or "You have a big problem with me" or "What is your problem?" These types of beginning show defensiveness and the conversation is doomed.

Concentrate on effects

Show how the impoliteness has affected you. "Dan, when I am making an important point; you often interrupt me, and I have to start again to make my point. This is happening repeatedly and trying my patience. I'd appreciate if you didn't interrupt me. You can speak when I am finished."

Keep above it

Some people can only hurt people with their words, but when people reply, they can't take it. They reply abusively. So don't give up your advantage of professionalism. Once you go down to their level and respond with equal abrasiveness, you have given away your power. If you have nothing productive to say, walk away with dignity and come back later.

Ask questions

Suppose you have asked someone at the workplace to stop disrespectful remarks about your weight. For example, you can say you don't like to call "Fatso" or "Baby Elephant." The other person may say, "Come on! It is just a joke. You are too sensitive." You can reply by saying, "I don't see the issue this way. I don't appreciate name calling. Please stop this behavior." Listen to what the other person has to say and reply, "Whether I am too sensitive or not, these nicknames disturb me, and hurt my feelings. I appreciate if you call me by my name instead."

When you have done the wrong deed

Everyone can be rude, occasionally, so if you do it accidentally, you need to apologize. A genuine apology can keep a customer coming back or mend a working relationship with a coworker. An apology consists of three parts:

- Acknowledgment (It was I who did it)

- Expression of regret (I am sorry)

- Promise not to repeat (It won't happen again)

Chapter 6 Workplace Disputes

When a diverse group of people works in a closed environment for long hours daily; then work stress, unclear and deadlines can create conflict. It is common that workplace disputes will take place. You can either be part of it or help manage it.

Is it a disagreement or a fight?

Constructive disagreement is not a bad thing. It can result in better products and services and innovative solutions to complex problems. Disagreement forces an examination of ideas, options, and decisions. Useful disagreement includes:

- Respect for boundaries.

- Reasoned support for a position.

- Discussion around clearly defined expectations.

Discussion around clearly defined expectations

"In today's meeting, I would like to discuss our promotional campaign for the next quarter. We already have the reports from our consultants; now let's see what others have to say. I want to hear everyone's point." This message triggers a lively dialogue between coworkers.

Reasoned support for a position

It is important to hear every staff member, but the final decision must be taken based on data and facts. Those who are arguing and disagreeing should be able to say why they are not in agreement, and they should back up their arguments with facts and reasons.

Respect for boundaries

Disagreements should be frank, honest, and candid. However, there is no reason for arguments to become snipping about gender, age, race or sexual orientation. This type of conversation should be stopped immediately by team members or team leader. A statement such as "I disagree with this design because ......" is far different from "This idea is a complete nonsense; it won't work in a million years"

Why people fight

Disarmament is healthy, but fights can blow up around issues that are related to the day-to-day workings of the company. One of the interesting causes of conflict relates to a particular type of change – a promotion. When you get promoted, you may have to discuss some issue with your subordinates (who were your coworkers before). A conversation example:

- You: "Richard, it came to my attention that you are not comfortable working under me. You have discussed the issue with others."

- Richard: "I don't have a problem. I had the same qualification as you, but you got the promotion, and I didn't." (So Richard told you that what is the problem).

- You: "Yes, it is true that you and I both have the same experience, but management liked my future proposal better than yours, so they promoted me. However, I would like to develop a good working relationship with you. How do you think we could make this situation better?"

- Richard: "We work for the same company, and we both want the same thing, how to get more sales. I would say the first thing you should do is you should talk less and listen more to others. Just because you are the manager, doesn't make you right always" (Maybe Richard's voice is a bit disrespectful).

- You: "I didn't know that I was listening less. I will remedy the issues promptly. Thank you for telling me this." (So you just overlooked Richard's impoliteness and went straight to the main issue).

- Richard: "Not a problem, you were a better listener before, but recently; you have developed a habit of not listening."

- You: "Yes, I will try to be aware of it. Now the other issue I wanted to talk to you. As you know, we are opening two new branches next December. I highly value your contributions and want your input on this matter."

- Richard: "I am working on my report and submit it next week with a detailed plan on how to provide better service through those upcoming branches."

- You: "Ok, I am counting on you."

- Richard: "Thank you for trusting me with this important issue."

So you can see you have done a good job by dodging unpleasant answers from Richard. On top of it, you engaged him; asked for his opinion and show him that you trust his judgment and value his contribution. This is just one example, but in the real world, you have to confront many Richard several times and deal with different issues.

Chapter 7 Dealing with Bad Bosses

Dealing with good bosses is easier and some are dreadful and difficult to work with.

The most common bad bosses and how to handle them

There are different types of bad bosses. They include:

- The micromanager

- The inexperienced boss

- The tentative boss

- The explosive boss

- The bully boss

Managing the micromanager

Micromanaging bosses get to the top because of a variety of reasons. They are promoted because they are good at what they do. However, the ability to supervise and manage others is not an inborn trait. If the boss has no training on how to manage their employees, then they won't do it very well. They will fall back into their comfort zone, which is questioning everything. Your boss will demand to overview every interview, see every picture and approve every word.

You may approach a boss like this saying: "You know; I can see how hard you work at managing others and noticing every detail. I want to help you relieve some of your pressure and take on some of the workloads. This will also help me to develop my skills at the same time. For example, you can give me the responsibility to oversee the opening of our new branch in the Bronx. I am very good at managing people and planning an event and won't let you down."

"How about this?" I will create my plan and show it to you. If you need any adjustments, we can do it. Then every other day, I will send you the detail report, and you can visit us every week to know the progress."

This regular check-in may be sufficient for your boss to allow you some freedom. You will not get full freedom overnight, but it is the first step. This approach works only when you do a really good job as promised. Noticing your good work, they might relinquish some of their control over you. On the other hand, if you fail or mismanage a few things, you will find them becoming more micromanaging.

The inexperienced boss

Bosses may be inexperienced because they are young and/or new in the position. The problem is worse when the new bosses don't receive any training on how to manage people. The important thing about dealing with an inexperienced boss is not to take advantage of him, instead focus on training them. You have to do this without indicating that he lacks a few things (which they are aware of already). You could ask:

- "What you want to achieve with this department? What are your short-term and long-term goals?"

- "How you measure success?"

- "How do you prefer to work? Do you like to delegate entire projects? Or do you like to handle the big picture and delegate details?"

- "If your employees have questions, do you want them to talk to you face-to-face or do you prefer email?"

- "Do you like to meet with managers individually? Or do you like frequent staff meetings?"

- "How can I help you to get acclimated with this department? I have been with this company for nine years, and I know how things work."

These questions will make the new manager think about how they want to run the department. With your assistance, you will notice a big improvement in their abilities. If you see your inexperienced boss is making a wrong move, you can advise how to approach it better.

Supporting the tentative boss

A tentative boss usually doesn't know what they want. They give consistent direction because of their opinion change with the organization and policies. Often staff members become confused because of the lack of leadership and direction, and they become demotivated and demoralized. Help your tentative boss by being decisive yourself and asking for details when they are needed. Actively ask for feedback and document it.

- "I will start the interviews for the annual report today. Can you tell me please when do you need the report? I can finish the interviews within a week."

- "Which image will you choose as a cover for this week's magazine? The African safari or the dessert adventure?"

- "What is your opinion on the last week's report? Is there anything that needs changing?"

Some bosses seem tentative, but actually, they are hands-off. They want to focus on their work while at the same time expect others to do their jobs. If you need clearer direction, you have to ask for what you want:

- "The client wants cash for his equipment. Several ways we can approach this, but I think a lease is the best option right now. What you think?"

- "What is the deadline for this project?" At this rate, we can finish within 10 days. Do you want us to finish sooner? If so, we will need more staff."

- "I need clearer direction on how you want us to work with the other team. Which one should deal with the clients and which one should focus on developing the plan?"

The bully boss

Bully boss is the worst of the bosses. Bullies threaten, abuse and demean. The call employees by nicknames and even threaten to physically harm them. Bullies bully because they can. Bullies revel in the uneven balance of power. Most of their excuses begin with the word "you":

"You made me lose my temper."

"You will stay all night if you have to. I need this by tomorrow."

"You are not calling the shots. I am."

Many employees don't want to stand up and confront a bully boss because they think it will make things worse. "What if I say this, and it makes things worse?" "What if he says an even worse thing, and I have to quit?"

Here is how you can deal with a boss, who is bullying you:

- Find out if others are suffering like you from their bullying behavior.

- Record every incident, including witnesses, date and the surrounding environment. Keep a record of your emails.

- Simply ask your bully boss to stop.

- If it is not possible for you to confront this person, then put your objection in writing.

- Doing meditation can help to calm you down.

- You can't make a legal claim about bullying, but if you documented everything, then you can make a dismissal claim against your boss.

Chapter 8 Communicating with Customers

Providing bad customer service can hurt you

When customers are not happy, they get angry. If the customers feel they are treated rudely, they:

- Go to the management

- Spread the word

Go to the management

Upper management cares about how customers are treated, and if they receive a well-reasoned phone call or carefully crafted letter of a complaint, they will investigate the incident.

Spread the word

The customers can damage the company by spreading the word how badly they were treated. You could probably lose a few potential clients because of that.

Behaviors that drive customers away

1. Not looking at or speaking to the customer: This type of behavior annoys the customer. For example, if you are purchasing groceries from a store and the clerk never looks at you or spoke to you, focusing only on ringing up the purchase and using your credit card, then you will get angry because of this rude behavior.

2. "No": This "no" word annoys customers.

    - Customer: "Do you have this item available in your stock?"

- Service person: "No"

- Customer: "Can you tell me when it will be available?"

- Service person: "No"

- Customer: "Do you have other brands similar to this?"

- Service person: "No"

Instead of sounding robotic, you could say, "I am sorry this item is out of the stock right now. If you want the item, we can make notes and call you when the item arrives." The customer will be annoyed that he didn't get the item he was looking for, but your helpfulness will encourage him to come back later.

3. "You have to understand": This type of answering is rude to the customers. Remember customers don't have to understand. The clients don't have to understand your company policy or your delivery schedule. The only thing they have to know is when they are going to get their item. So you can't say things like, "You have to understand that we only receive delivery once a week." It is better to say, "We are out of the item you want. We only get delivery once a week. If you want I can call our other stores to see if they have the item and can send it here."

4. Inappropriate behavior: These include talking on a phone while you are serving a customer; continuing a personal dialogue with another employee while the customer is present; eating or drinking during a conversation with a customer; chopping on a wad of

gum; or looking impatient when a customer has a question. If the customer has a choice, he will choose a vendor who is friendly, polite and professional.

5. Forgetting your manners: Customers entering your store should receive a pleasant welcome from everyone they encounter. Smile and say, "Welcome." Convey warmth and approachability with your body language. Don't be rigid and closed off. Appreciating the customer is a big part of customer service, and little things like thank you, encourage people to come to your store again.

Phone calls

- Customers can get angry when call center employees are incompetent and rude.

- Can you hold?: The customer will be angry if you put them on hold without getting their answer. Listen closely what the client says and have the courtesy to wait for an answer.

- What is your account number?: When a customer calls, don't start your conversation with like "Johnson Utility Company, may I have your account number?" Instead, start with "Good morning. What can I do for you?"

- Putting a customer on hold: If you must put a customer on hold while you work to resolve an issue, keep the wait time to a minimum. Ignoring a customer can make him go away, but he will be back, and he will be angry.

- Language issues: Overseas customer service can cause a language problem. If the representative doesn't speak English very well or has a heavy accent, then the customer will not get the proper service he is looking for. Here is an example:

Judy (customer): "I am expecting a check today or tomorrow. When it comes, I will come to your branch and make payment."

Representative: "So you will be mailing a check today?"

Judy: No, as I told you, I will get the check today or tomorrow and make payment tomorrow."

Rep: "You will make the payment today?"

Judy: "No. Please listen to what I am saying. Can I get another representative?"

Chapter 9 Practicing Tough Conversation

Deliberately position yourself in the tough conversation situations and boost your belief and confidence.

Deliberately place yourself in situations that triggers tough conversations:

- Say no: Say no if you don't want to do something. If someone what to you to donate some money, and you don't want to donate to that certain charity, say no. If your boss or coworker asks to do some extra work after the office hour, say no sometimes. If any of your friends want some favor that put you in a stressful situation, say no. Gently say no to your friends or colleagues and don't get into any quarrel.

- Return an item to the store: Return an item to the store; it may be a cloth, a book or some food item. In most cases, store authority will take it back without any questions ask, but sometimes you may encounter a negative response. This stressful situation will be help you practice tough conversation. Try returning items without a receipt or without the original packaging. Make things more stressful for you, the store authority may not take the item back, but the experience will help you to practice better.

- Ask someone else to change his behavior: Ask someone else to change his behavior. If your roommate leaves his or her dishes in the sink without cleaning, ask him or her not to do that. Practice this approach with strangers as well. If you are in a restaurant and someone is smoking, tell him to stop. Maybe someone is playing music loudly and disturbing everybody, walk up to him and tell him not to disturb everybody.

- Stay still even after the traffic light turns to green: Stay still for a few seconds, even after the traffic light turns to green. Drivers behind you will get frustrated and start yelling or honk their horns.

- Take extra time in lines: Take extra-long time when using bank deposit machines. Do several withdrawals, transfer funds, check receipt at a slow pace and let people wait for a long time behind you. When buying things from supermarkets; say you left your wallet in the car and don't have the money to pay for the items. If people are waiting behind you, make an extra effort to waste as much time as possible.

- Return food at restaurants: Return foods at restaurants, say it is overcooked or undercooked or maybe soup is cold. During service, create some cause and try to reject the food. Normally, restaurants will change your food accordingly, but the conversation will help you practice.

- Purposefully try to look stupid or make mistakes: When you feel you are better equipped to handle the tough conversation, do some things that make you look stupid.

- Draw attention to yourself: When shopping, knock over a display or some other items and draw attention to yourself. Don't do things that are out of control, stay within the limit and do small unusual things.

These small incidents will help you practice tough conversations.

Conclusion

Often managers, employees, and even bosses dread tough conversations. This is a straightforward, no-nonsense guide that shows both managers and employees how to have tough conversations and achieve a satisfactory result. Packed with practical and pragmatic suggestions and methods of dealing with the tough stuff at work, this helpful book features simple strategies that you can put to use immediately.